Setting the Church on Fire

Serving and Leading the Church in the Modern World

Bill Huebsch

Sanctus Press

290 Dayton Ave
Suite 3E
St Paul, MN 55102

Cover art by Mark Hakomaki.
http://www.markhakomaki.com/

ISBN: 9781083017710

Acknowledgments

I am indebted to Bill McDonough, Assistant Professor of Theology at The College of St. Catherine in St. Paul, Minnesota, for permission to use portions of the research he did into the life and contributions of Bishop Ray Lucker. *Raymond A. Lucker (1927-2001): Bishop-herald of Catechesis for Conversion in an Adult Church*" (March 2007).

I am indebted to Jim Collins, author of *Good to Great* (New York: HarperCollins, 2001) whose insights into business, presented in that book are applied here with certain adaptations directly to Catholic parish pastoral planning.

Introduction

Did you ever know someone with dreams and visions for the Church? Many people have them, and I'll bet you're one! If so, you take your place alongside women and men of all nations and races whose dreams and visions have been shaping the Church for centuries.

Pope St John XXIII had dreams and visions for the Church, too. His dream was to set the Church on fire! And his vision was that laypeople, as well as clergy and religious, should do this work. They were taken up and given lofty expression at the Second Vatican Council. His dreams led others to dream with him, and after him, Popes St Paul VI, St John Paul II, and Benedict XVI had visions as well. In this moment of history, Pope Francis has expressed perhaps the most pastoral dreams of all. The popes, of course, are only servants of the Church, the People of God. And the People of God have dreams and visions, too. You'll be reading about all of these dreamers in this book.

This book is a guide to help you move in the direction of the dreams and visions that you have for your parish, but you may very well never actually finish! As you will see in this book, the process of turning dreams and visions into specific pastoral programs of welcome, mercy, compassion, and healing never comes to an end.

Good or Great?

In the introduction to his powerful book, *Good to Great,* (New York: HarperCollins, 2001) Jim Collins wrote, "Good is the enemy of great. And that is one of the key reasons why we have so little that becomes great."

He's so correct! And for Catholic parishes, this is a powerful wake-up call. The Church is filled with "good" parishes: The liturgies are planned. The education programs use a nice looking book. Some of the people take an active role in parish leadership and ministry. The collections pay the bills for the most part. People can get their children baptized without too much hassle. The second-grade students receive their first communions as they do every year. Couples getting married go through their routine of meetings. Lent comes, and Easter follows, and sometime around Pentecost, things slow down for summer. It's a "good" parish.

But can we really afford to keep focusing only on being good? The world is bigger than that in every direction, more challenging and more dynamic! And it needs the message we have to bring! We have, after all, the secret of the Reign of God, and we need to be more than merely "good" to announce that. We need to move toward becoming *great!*

Time after time in his daily homilies, public appearances, and formal documents, Pope Francis has called the Church to greatness—as Spirit-filled disciples, as agents of healing, as accompanists, evangelizers, and pastors.

Setting the Church on fire!

In a great parish, the liturgy will not only be planned, but a team of leaders will also plan how to increase from mediocre to fantastic both 1) the level of participation and 2) the sense of welcome. In a great parish, the education process will not only use a good textbook, but over time, a team of leaders will plan ways to provide faith formation for *all* members, including adults. Leaders will coach parents to become the real teachers of their own children. In a great parish, not only will there be some people actively involved, but a team of leaders will plan ways to gradually engage more and more people in parish life, by lighting a fire in people's hearts through encounters with Christ. In a great parish, not only will the collections pay the bills, but a team of leaders will gradually see collections rise to the point where the parish can afford more, not only for itself but also for the poor, the care of the earth, and immigrants. In a great parish, not only will children and young people celebrate the sacraments, or couples prepare to marry, but a team of leaders will plan how to place those preparing for sacraments in the context of the whole community, and the catechumenate will be the inspiration and empowerment behind it all! In a great parish, catechists and teachers will be in ongoing formation, creating a spiritual community at the hearts of our schools and parishes.

The Core Work in Pastoral Ministry

When we speak of core work in pastoral theology, we refer to that ministry which introduces people to the person of Jesus Christ and helps them learn to walk with him as their friend. Such friendship with Jesus is the basic core of everything in the Church. We know that we are sinners. We only need to reflect briefly on our lives up to this point to see the many ways in which we have been selfish, cruel, dishonest, indifferent to suffering, turning a blind eye to the poor, and clinging with all our might to our own money.

The core work of the Church is to help people come to believe that we are forgiven. Because of the self-giving love of Christ and by the grace of God, we are forgiven. God's mercy is larger than all our sins combined.

Therefore, the core work to be done in a great parish requires that a team of leaders will gradually build up a process by which members have either 1) that initial encounter with Christ and his life-changing friendship and forgiveness, or 2) deeper communion with him through retreats, the sacraments, and faith sharing. Little by little in a great parish, a fire will be lit! Little by little, a team of leaders will help move the parish forward, not merely to repeat this year what they did last, but to move forward in a consistent direction of ever-deeper faith over a long time. They will build momentum gradually until one day, a few years from now, everyone will stop and look back and say, "Gosh, we're really a *great parish*, aren't we?"

Great parishes aren't built by simply following after the latest pastoral trends! They aren't built in one or two or three years. It takes a lot of effort and a team of modest yet driven leaders to shift from being good to being on the road to greatness, as Jim Collins reminds us in his book. There is no one plan or one action or one program to adopt that can make a parish great. But there is a direction, and that direction is deep friendship with Jesus lived out in parish life.

So rather than suggesting big new programs to implement, *Setting the Church on Fire* suggests moving in the constant direction of lifelong growth by establishing a pattern of movement, step-by-step, little by little. *Setting the Church on Fire* suggests a strong plan of formation for the whole community, but it also cautions you not to run off in several directions at once. The core work is quite simple, and we keep returning to it constantly. It's the concept that comes to us from the popes and bishops, but also directly from the Gospel. And that core work, of course, is the center point of *Setting the Church on Fire*. Every single dimension of pastoral ministry suggested here always leads to and from this core: to help people experience an initial encounter with Christ and to grow into deeper communion with God. It is to turn one's heart toward Christ and be converted. However you name it, there is one central vision here: *Help people deepen their communion with Christ, and you will light a fire in your parish!* That is the dream and vision of this book.

Through discipline and consistency, we will gradually build up our good parishes into great ones by growing the number of people who are on fire with the love of Christ and each other! Once the momentum begins, the movement will sustain itself. All the parish leaders have to do is stoke the fire and keep out of the way!

We sometimes settle for so little as parish workers and members! We're willing to accept the modest goal of balancing a budget or not making anyone angry in the parish! What is that about? It's about safety and security. But growing the parish requires risk, danger, and maybe even our very lives! It requires us to go out on a limb. It requires us to do what St John XXIII did when he was inspired to call Vatican II. The idea of a council, he later said, appeared to him "like a flash of heavenly light." He trusted that flash, and in his own modest yet determined way, he changed the course of history and all our lives as well.

A flash of heavenly light
Now the task is upon us. Don't settle for being merely a good parish. Don't pass from one year to the next repeating

the same pleas for engagement on the part of your members. Don't sit back and wait for the ones coming after you to do this. Step forward now and move your parish from being good to being truly great!

We as a Church can do so much more to announce the reign of God! We Catholics have a true heart for the poor; we love the liturgical flow of the year; we believe in defending the rejected and the forgotten. We're big enough to embrace everyone, and we really know how to bury the dead! There's just nothing quite like a Catholic funeral!

And yet, so many pastoral staff people in these "good parishes" complain that attendance is dropping among the young, that collections are too low to meet the demands, that it's harder and harder to recruit volunteers, that we have lost our moral voice in the culture, that we're busy arguing over the language of our rituals while the world is marching to war! We're not working at our core work: helping people meet Christ. We're distracted by politics, rubrics, or our own fears.

Setting the Church on Fire provides a road map toward a new horizon, one that is promised to us by Christ in the Spirit. So let's get busy and become great!

Chapter 1:
What is the Vision
of the Church?

"Vision without action is merely a dream.
Action without vision just passes the time.
Vision with action can change the world."
Joel A. Barker

Many people are working in parish leadership these days, and you're probably one of them. People like you are the backbone of the Church. You are of good heart and strong faith. The Church has never had so many talented, willing, and able leaders! And parish leaders are working today in this new millennium at a unique moment in Church history. We're in a period of great, historic restoration of certain ancient practices of the Church, many of which had been out of use for centuries!

One of these ancient practices now being renewed and restored is the catechumenate. That term "catechumenate" is one that unfortunately isn't meaningful yet to many

Catholics. It is a word of Greek origin, and it refers in general to that process through which newcomers to the faith prepare for baptism, confirmation, and Eucharist. Sometimes we refer to it by its liturgical name, the Rite of Christian Initiation of Adults, or RCIA.

However, we refer to it, the practices of the catechumenate are very important to the modern Church. They are the bedrock forms of catechesis from which the entire Church benefits. When we speak about catechesis (another word of Greek origin!) we refer of course to the passing on of the faith from one generation to the next, or even among members of the same generation. "Catechesis" means, literally, "to echo the faith" or to allow faith to be evident in one's life, so much so that others see in us what we see in Christ.

"Others see in us what we see in Christ," the love, sacrifice, and joy that are hallmarks of the followers of Jesus. Others can see that in us, and when they do, they too may become followers of Christ. That's catechesis in its truest form.

Whole community or family catechesis
When we speak today about whole community catechesis, we mean that this echoing of the faith, this *catechesis*, is not meant only for children, but also for adults in the Church. It's meant for the *whole community*. Really, it's that simple. And the method by which we provide catechesis for adults grows out of the catechumenate we were discussing just now. The practices of the catechumenate provide a powerful and effective way for us to help adults grow in their faith.

Others see Christ in us when we echo our faith
The reason we turn to the catechumenate like this is that many of us adult Catholics in today's Church, at least in

western nations such as the United States, England, Canada, Ireland, and others, have indeed already been baptized. Most of us were actually baptized as infants. But many of us have not had any faith formation, or any religious education, or any catechesis, or any intentional growth in our faith since those childhood religion classes in the parish or school.

Because of that, we are somewhat like those people who join the Church for the first time, and we are therefore in need of the kind of faith formation the catechumenate offers. The catechumenate has four stages. 1) Newcomers first pass through an initial inquiry and introduction to the faith. 2) When ready, they publicly state their intentions to the Church and enter the catechumenate, which is actually stage two of the process. In this stage, they are introduced in more depth to the doctrine, prayer life, and mission of the Church. During stage two, they are provided an accompanist or sponsor, an already-committed Christian, who walks with them on their journey of faith. 3) When they are ready (there is no pre-determined length of time for stage two) they request baptism and celebrate their initiation into Christ at the Easter Vigil of that year. 4) After Easter, they enter into a period known as mystagogy, during which they reflect on all that has happened and allow it to live more fully in their hearts.

The entire experience is one whose center-point is conversion to Christ and deepening communion with him. The study of doctrine or church customs, or prayer and spirituality, all follow on that. Conversion precedes catechesis.

Today, because of the strong work of Pope John Paul II in this regard, it is widely understood that all of us Catholics need to deepen our communion with Christ. We need to grow in our love of Scripture. We need to share with each other our journeys of faith. And we need some outright instruction in what it means to be fully Catholic. These are basically the same needs being met in the catechumenate each year. But of course, we can't ask all the adults of the Church to re-enter the catechumenate. So in whole community catechesis, *we take elements of that catechumenate and implant them in the rest of parish life.* In a nutshell, this is what we mean by whole community catechesis: the process of implanting in parish life the ancient elements of the catechumenate:

- retreats,
- breaking open the Word,
- encounters,
- small communities of growing faith,
- adult faith gatherings,
- liturgical experiences,
- a strong focus on Triduum and the paschal mystery,
- living as households of faith,
- and catechists who are formed for life.

The results of doing this are phenomenal! Already-baptized adults grow in their own faith, seeing Christ as the center of their lives and the Church as the community of God. The children's program is much stronger because now the parents are also involved. And the whole parish has more volunteers, more money, more goodwill, and more vibrant liturgies! It's a win-win-win-win situation.

In whole community catechesis, there is formation in faith, conscience, spirituality, morality, and prayer. This is more than mere *information.* Formation like this involves the whole person, beyond the cognitive. It rises out of an encounter with Christ. It leads to conversion of the heart, to a shift in horizons from following rules and avoiding eternal punishment, to active loving, working for justice, and integrating faith into life. Knowing *about* religion is one thing, but encountering Christ and living the resulting faith is another. It is this latter encounter with its resultant change of heart that catechesis today seeks to encourage and promote.

Chapter 2
Who Makes this Vision Happen?

"Your vision will become clear
only when you look into your heart.
Who looks outside dreams.
Who looks inside, awakens."
Anonymous

So, who are you? Are you a lay volunteer leader? A parish priest? A paid pastoral associate? On the staff of a parish school? A volunteer minister in the liturgy or education or pastoral care programs of the parish? As you prepare for this work of pastoral ministry, it's important to be aware of your own role in the parish. Read these profiles (read them all, even those not about you) and take a few minutes to get in touch with your own thoughts. These are meant to stimulate you to be clear about your own experience and beliefs about your parish.

Are you a parish leader?

In today's Catholic parish, the number of those who are actively engaged with parish life seems to be getting smaller, but you're still engaged yourself. You're a parish leader, helping shape parish life by planning programs and managing budgets and facilities. You're on the parish council, or a finance committee, or some other parish leadership group. You were elected or appointed to this role, and you might even feel that you aren't fully prepared to help lead the parish as you're expected to do. You probably attend many meetings, each with its own agenda. It's frustrating for you sometimes because you sense that the people of the parish are rather indifferent to all that the parish offers. They don't seem to care about the need for a steady stream of income, or about the need to update the buildings, or the need to be actively engaged themselves.

And most likely the other members of the committee or council of which you're a part don't prepare for the meetings very well or don't even attend them all. Like you, they're busy. Maybe they travel for their work, or commute a long distance daily, or have many family demands. As a result, the meetings aren't always terribly effective. And furthermore, your role is simply to *advise* the parish priest, not to make the final decisions, and you sometimes feel that isn't a very essential thing to do—merely advise someone else.

The parish may have a difficult time filling all the leadership posts, and even though you have thought of resigning, you have agreed to stay on and keep plugging away. Good for you!

A lot of good things do happen in the parish, and a lot of people do have their spiritual needs met by the parish every week. So even though the parish isn't perfect, it's pretty darn good, and you're glad to be part of it all.

You personally know many households that aren't active in the parish anymore. Who knows why? Maybe their faith just grew cold. Maybe it's a second or even a third marriage, and they don't feel very welcome. Maybe they're living together without the benefit of marriage at all and feel that the Church condemns them for it. Maybe they gave up on the Church as the abuse crisis deepened. Or maybe they're using a method of birth control that the Church doesn't approve, and they just can't reconcile themselves to being active. They probably haven't had any adult faith development since they were in grade school, so they may have a mistaken idea about what the Church teaches. Or maybe one of the members of the household isn't Catholic. It can be tough to remain active when your husband or wife isn't. And parishes aren't always very welcoming to non-Catholic spouses.

Most likely some of these "inactive" Catholics are your own family members, your children or siblings. You might actually feel a little hurt that they're not still faithful Catholics. It's close to home for you

And yet, you're a parish leader. You've chosen to stay and make this parish stronger. You've got dreams and visions for your parish. You want the parish to be more welcoming for all these people. You want your parish to somehow become a magnet that attracts them back. You want to offer people mercy and compassion, to be understanding about how people have suffered. You're searching for an effective way to do this, a pastoral plan for the parish that helps people get active again.

Are you a volunteer minister?

In today's parish, the number of people being invited to serve in a public ministry of the Church is growing every year, and you are one of these people. You're a volunteer worker, called on to provide a specific ministry, which fifty years ago would have been done exclusively by the priests or sisters. So this means you are volunteering your time and giving your talents in liturgy, or youth ministry, or education, or visiting the sick or homebound, or working in ministries for the poor, or the rejected. Or you might be one of the money counters in the parish or one of the funeral ministers. Or you're working in one of a dozen other parish ministries.

Because you're actively engaged yourself in parish life, you may have a hard time understanding why more people aren't more active. When new volunteers are needed, you sometimes try to recruit them yourself so you know how difficult it can be. People are busy! They have lots of demands on their time, and more often than not, the parish is a somewhat low priority for them.

It might even be possible in your parish that the group of volunteers working in music ministry, for example, or in religious education, or on the school fundraising committee is basically the same as it's been for many years. You might even have inadvertently formed a sort of clique that newcomers find hard to penetrate. New people might feel inhibited to suggest new ideas for fear they'll be told that in this parish, it has been tried before and failed, so new ideas aren't welcome anymore.

It's great to have you volunteering your time, and since no one else seems to step forward, the parish really needs you to continue.

And yet, new ideas might sometimes help. Like the parish leaders described above, you can also see that fewer people seem active in the parish these days. You would like to attract more people to get involved, but it's a catch-22. To make room for new folks, you have to step aside a little. But you have a certain way of doing things, and you can't really step aside until someone else learns that, but new people might want to do things differently, so change comes very slowly or not at all.

Every once in a while, the staff person who manages the ministry in which you're involved, be it a lay worker, a sister, or the parish priest, asks you to attend a training day somewhere in the diocese or archdiocese. Or maybe the training is being offered right there at your own parish. In either case, this means giving more time to the parish, and time is something you might not have a lot of right now.

But still, father or sister or the lay staff person has told you how important it is to attend these continuing education days, and you are interested in the topic. Many of the other volunteers can't attend for one reason or another, so you do go. The room gradually fills up with volunteers, parish staff people, and a handful of parish priests, all from other parishes. The diocesan or archdiocesan staff is also there. A couple of publishers may have display tables set up, probably because they put up the money to bring in the speaker or pay for the lunch.

Finally, the event gets underway. There's a rather long morning prayer, followed by some announcements, and then the speaker is introduced. He's written a couple of books about the topic being addressed, and he's got a PowerPoint presentation running and a flip chart ready to go. You might think to yourself, "If this person's not very good, I'm leaving at noon." A lot of people are actually thinking the same thing.

The first thing this speaker does is to ask a question of the group. "What do you want the outcome of all your efforts to be in your parish? What do you want people to take away from their encounter with the parish? *What do you want to happen as a result of your ministry?*" The whole group sitting in that hall is silent. It's a tough question. So the speaker, who has a sense of humor, says, "This isn't a rhetorical question. I'm expecting someone to answer me." A little laughter and the group is relaxing a little. Bit by bit, the speaker teases out of the group, including you, what outcomes you hope for in your ministry and writes them on that flip chart:

1. More people to be active
2. People to *want* to learn about faith
3. More participation in the liturgy for the parish
4. People to know Christ
5. Parishioners to actually live their faith
6. Parents to get involved with their kids' faith
7. More volunteers
8. And so forth

As you sit there, you really hope this speaker can help you do this. Because yes, this is exactly what your own dreams and visions for the parish are. It actually helps to hear that people from all these other parishes have the same dreams and visions too. What is the pastoral plan that can deliver this? And how can you take it home to your own parish and implement it? That's the thousand-dollar question, isn't it?

Are you the parish priest?
The last twenty years have not been an easy time to be the parish priest. But here you are, Father. For better or worse, you're the one in charge. You're probably working too

hard. Many weeks end up being longer than you planned, even if you have a day off scheduled. A funeral is a funeral, after all. They certainly can't be scheduled very far in advance. And since most of the work you do is behind the scenes, with the sick or dying or during the weekdays when most parishioners can't see what's happening in the parish, there are most likely some people who think you're not working hard enough!

And for another thing, you simply can't please everybody. Some parishioners are demanding more pious devotional opportunities. Others want more work for social justice. Some want both. A third group just seems to disagree with many Church teachings and is angry if you even mention the place of women in the Church or the fact that the parish hasn't bought a new hymnal in almost twenty years. So you tread lightly, not wanting to offend anyone, trying to keep everyone happy.

But it's not easy. You stand in the middle and often take hits from everyone. What you want is not very complicated: you want people to be active and involved, to sing at Sunday Mass, to increase their contributions a little, to support the building fund, to get along during parish meetings, to even be there to attend those meetings in the first place, and to love the Church.

And you also want to make a lasting contribution to this parish. You know that eventually you'll be transferred, but it is important that the pastoral life of this parish be strong. You want to leave it in good shape, and you really want to make a contribution to the lives of the folks here in this parish. So you're seeking a pastoral plan to help you do that.

What keeps you up nights is that you know full well that 60 or 70 percent of parents are simply not involved in their kid's religious education. It isn't so much that they're of poor heart or bad intent (most of them want to be good parents, after all) but the Church or the parish school has been providing only children's programs for so long that there just isn't any way for these parents to be part of it. The only exception is first reconciliation and first Eucharist preparation; they are part of that. And what you see then is how really disoriented most of those parents really are about everything having to do with the Church.

And you know that once they've been confirmed, that crowd of young people is going to disappear. As their parish priest, you hope they'll come back one day, but you feel almost powerless to hang on to them now.

You know that it's tough to reach out to the divorced and remarried, a large number in your parish. And yet, you know also that those first marriages were often entered into when they were just kids—too young really—and now here they are, finally married to someone wonderful for them, living in a real "holy bond" but, of course, it's a marriage which the Church doesn't bless. You're inclined to defend the new and real bonds of marriage in which they're now living, but you also know you can't.

Then there are those others who are living outside the norm of the Church. You want to welcome them without appearing to break the rules. You know that people are inactive for a reason, be it their disagreement with the Church, or a lack of an initial encounter with Christ, or the result of a mixed marriage, or that they simply wandered away slowly and now don't have a clue how to return. And after people have been away from actively practicing their faith for a while, it's tough to find an avenue back. At the moment the pastoral plan for these inactive ones is that they're supposed to pick up their phone and call you as parish priest to make an appointment to go to confession. Technically, they're living in sin. The way back is to confess and get absolution, a long-standing pastoral practice of the Church.

But you know most people aren't going to do that. In fact, they might be inactive in part *because* of confession. A lot of people fear this sacrament and not very many people participate in it, including the active Catholics. So as a pastoral plan, you are very aware that this simply isn't enough.

This situation: so many inactive people with no real plan to get them re-engaged with their faith; this is what keeps you up at night. Your own dreams and visions for the parish have to do with helping these folks find an avenue home.

Every now and then, someone on the bishop's staff sends out a notice about a training day for liturgists or catechists or even for the whole parish staff. If you have the day free and no funeral comes up, you can attend. But quite honestly, what's going to change if you do attend and listen to some speaker explain a new approach to this or that? You've been down that road before and tried everything.

There's been a lot of talk in recent years about the need for accompaniment, mercy, and compassion for people, about the need to help adults discern what God may be asking of them. Even though the ideas are good ones, and you support these ideas in theory, you wonder how to put it into practice. How do you get people to take part in something that they just don't seem interested in? The best ideas in the world don't help if people aren't interested.

And what really hurts and bothers you is that some families who were formerly in your parish have actually found a home in another denomination. They were invited by a neighbor or friend to start attending the Glory of God Community Church around the corner, and now they go there every week, contributing time and money to this more evangelical community. Why? What is that church offering to them that you aren't? It isn't so much that you feel competitive with this other denomination, but that you know we Catholics have a major contribution to make in people's lives, and it frustrates you when someone in the parish simply goes elsewhere.

So back to what we said earlier. As a parish priest, you really do want to help people grow in their faith. You want to help them become more active in parish life. You want them to know Christ and love the Church. But what's the pastoral plan to help you do this? You need a new approach, but it has to really work this time.

Are you a lay or religious pastoral associate? Or are you a deacon?

The day-to-day work of our Catholic parishes is increasingly being put into the hands of lay or religious men and women along with deacons. If you're one of them, you probably have done some advanced study of theology and are well prepared for the work you do. Your commitment is clear because you work long hours at a rather low wage, but you aren't doing it for the money in the first place. You're in this ministry because you believe that the Church needs you and that the people around you need a strong, effective parish community.

Like the others we have described here—leaders, ministry volunteers, or parish priests—you struggle to keep people engaged. And for you, this is very personal. This is your job, after all. This is what you've dedicated your life to, and you want others to be just as committed as you are. Like the parish priest (and maybe you're acting as in that role, depending on the parish) you're so busy amid weekly ministry needs that it's hard to see the bigger picture. It's hard to look beyond your own very busy ministry to consider a larger pastoral plan that would engage the whole parish.

And, even though you don't intend for this to happen, you do have to spend a little time and energy defending your own turf in the parish. After all, you do have a ministry area for which you're responsible, be it liturgy or religious education or pastoral care or administration. You can't just let go of this and assume someone else will get things done. And you have your core group of volunteers, which you have carefully cultivated and trained, and you don't want to do anything to upset them or make them think they aren't needed.

You get a lot of mail from the diocesan or archdiocesan pastoral center, not to mention from a host of Catholic publishers. You're often invited to attend this or that day of enrichment, or formation, or training, or whatever. From time to time, you do take part in these days, but you return home to your parish office, look through the mail, answer a few phone calls, and get ready for the event that evening— and to be honest, from year to year, not that much changes, despite what the guest speaker had to say. It's great to consider new ideas, but in the end, someone has to get the work done. You can't just let it all go and focus on every new idea that comes along.

But gnawing at the back of your mind is the reality in the Church today that many people really do not believe the Church loves them and supports them. They take only a minimal part in parish life, getting their kids into religious ed or through the sacraments, but not feeling deeply committed—and also not giving much time or money to parish needs. You know these people, better maybe than anyone, because you see them when they have needs. You're gracious with them, welcoming, inviting, but for some reason, they remain at the edge of parish life. Your own dreams and visions for the parish have to do with helping get such people re-engaged. But how?

Chapter 3
What Do Church Leaders Want Us to Do?

"You see things; and you say, 'Why?'
But I dream things that never were;
and I say, 'Why not?'"
George Bernard Shaw

One way to know the answer to this question is to turn to the papal and other universal or international Catholic meetings, documents, and statements. Another is to look at what the bishops of any given nation have set down as a direction for that particular local Church. And a third is to look at the activities and developments of the faithful who are working in universities, diocesan offices, and parishes.

We're going to do that here in a quick survey of all that's been happening in the years since 1960. But first—spoiler alert! —let's turn to "the back of the book" and look at the ending. What you'll find is that these have been the most dynamic and exciting years of renewal in the Church since the early centuries of the Church's founding. There has been enormous activity surrounding catechesis and liturgy—study weeks, synods of bishops, papal documents, conferences of bishops' statements, a major new catechism, the restoration of the catechumenate, renewal movements, youth ministry development, more papal documents, more study, whole university programs created to study all of this, and conference after conference after conference. And in the second decade of this millennium, along came Pope Francis calling the Church to new life. We've seen nothing like this in the Church in all of its history!

The new sense of direction which is emerging from all this has the power to really effectively announce the Reign of God, to provide a true spiritual home for people of all nations, and to chart the course for justice and peace that is the dream of the Gospels. Indeed, as you will see here, the strong work since the 1960s provides a clear sense of direction for the Church. But we all have to be ready to embrace the change in parish structure needed to bring this about. Whatever role you play, the work of implementing this bold new sense of direction, this bold new pastoral plan, falls now to you.

The 1960s
On the eve of the Second Vatican Council, the pastoral plan of the Church seemed quite simple. Bishops and parish priests provided all the leadership, while sisters and brothers handled the education and health care systems of the Church. Lay people attended Mass weekly, followed the moral and devotional direction set for them by the leaders, and used the sacrament of confession to reconcile themselves when they went astray.

Catechesis was based solely on the *Roman Catechism* from 1566 where answers to specific questions of faith and doctrine were memorized, along with prayers, lists, and other details of Catholic life. By and large in the United States, Canada, England, Wales, and Ireland, Catholics lived what was known as a "Catholic life." Everyday life was imbued with Catholic customs, beliefs, and traditions. So much was this the case that "catechism class" (as it was known in some parts of the Church) had only a very small gap to fill. The actual instruction was done through all the other means: home life, devotions, traditions, personal piety, fasting, abstinence, obedience to church norms, and of course, weekly confession and Mass attendance.

The pastoral plan for parishes had remained essentially the same since the sixteenth century. There had been so little change in fact during those four or five hundred years between Trent and Vatican II that when the bishops and theologians at Vatican II did begin to reform the Church, it came as quite a shock to many people. Having been held in place so long by the sheer force of the discipline of the Church's leaders and the threat of Hell, that old "Catholic life" now began to unravel and the need for a more vigorous catechesis became strong. These reforms came at just the right moment in our history because the culture around us was changing too but at an even faster rate.

Vatican II
Vatican II called for "full, active and conscious participation in the liturgy." The Council was calling for laypeople to engage the world and contribute to it from their faith, to animate that world with the Spirit of Christ. Vatican II spoke about a universal call to holiness. Vatican II led us toward charitable and prayerful ecumenical and interfaith relationships and dialogue. Vatican II described conscience as the place where we are alone with God whose voice echoes in our depths. Vatican II restored the catechumenate, which had not been active in the Church for

nearly seventeen hundred years. Vatican II restored our understanding of baptism as the essential sacerdotal sacrament.

But in fact, as the Council came to a close, the Church did not have a tradition of catechesis to help people learn and embrace all of this powerful work of the Spirit. It had only catechisms to memorize. Memorization is certainly part of any form of learning, but no one would seriously argue that it is sufficient to have mere cognitive recognition of doctrine and tradition.

Today we understand that there must also be a strong element of the emotive and intuitive in faith formation. The heart must be committed to Christ if one's faith is to be strong. We do not, after all, place our faith in the Church itself. The Church is not God. It's not enough to merely know *about* one's faith or church. Knowing about the Church doesn't make you Christian. For example, it's possible to study Judaism thoroughly: the prayers, prophets, history, traditions, rituals, people—all of it. That would not make you a Jew. So it is with Christianity. What makes us Christian is an encounter with the risen Christ, God's own son, revealing God's own heart to us.

At Vatican II, not much debate about catechesis was held. It was generally agreed at that time that we did not do very adequate catechesis within the Church. In fact, the catechumenate itself had fallen out of use, almost entirely. In the history of the Church, one struggles to find meaningful references to catechumenal practice after the fourth century or so. And with the advent of modern times, the Church addressed mainly the catechetical needs of children after baptism. It centered this catechetical work on preparation for the sacraments, which in time came to act almost like graduation. Once a person had been confirmed, he or she was finished with faith formation. Indeed, parishes helped create this thinking by offering almost no formal faith formation for anyone older than secondary school age.

The Church had long hoped to engage all adults in the catechetical process. And in fact, we have come to realize now that the primary aim of such catechesis in the Church is conversion, not instruction. But Vatican II itself, as it turned out, would not be the moment in our history where the needed development of catechesis would happen. In fact, at the Council, the only direct reference to catechesis comes in article forty-four of the "Decree on the Pastoral Office of Bishops in the Church." There it calls for a series of "general directories" to be drawn up after the Council. These were to address, for example, the care of souls, the pastoral care of special groups, "and also a directory for the catechetical instruction of the Christian people in which the fundamental principles of this instruction and its organization will be dealt with…"

Movements afoot
The Council Fathers were aware that already afoot throughout the world was a catechetical renewal. The search was already underway "for a better method than the questions and answers of the catechism," as Sr. Kate Dooley pointed out in an essay published in *The Echo Within* (Notre Dame: Ave Maria Press, 1997). In the early 1900s, catechetical leaders meeting in southern Germany were testing new methods. They recognized that merely knowing facts about the faith was not the same as encountering Christ and hearing the Gospel proclaimed!

The so-called "kerygmatic movement" of the 1950s went even further, moving us "to recapture the spirit and vision of the Church of the apostolic and patristic era" (Dooley).

This movement added the element of "formation" to the memorized catechism. Learners received the proclamation of the Gospel, the teachings of Jesus, and the saving acts of his life, death, and resurrection.

This movement was based on "four signs" that were to be in balance for a proper understanding of the faith:
- Liturgy
- Scripture
- Church teaching
- The witness of Christian living.

"Catechesis was no longer limited to instruction and to the classroom" (Dooley). Instead, it merged with liturgy, biblical study, and discipleship into an organic whole, just as it was experienced in the early Church. We are grateful to Josef Jungmann SJ (1889-1975), who taught pastoral theology on the faculty of the University of Innsbruck, for these insights which are becoming part and parcel of all effective catechesis today.

In the United States, Jungmann's work was popularized by Jesuit and religion educator Johannes Hofinger (1905-1984). It was mainly by Hofinger's efforts that a series of international catechetical study weeks were held in
- Nijmegen, 1959
- Eichstatt, 1960
- Bangkok, 1962
- Katigondo, 1964
- Manila, 1967
- Medellin, 1968.

These study weeks, as you can see, anticipated Vatican II and continued during and after it. They had an influence on the Council itself. The Eichstatt week had particular influence as it laid out principles of liturgical and catechetical renewal. But it was at Medellin, Columbia in 1968 that serious reflection on evangelization led to a new focus. It was seen during the week in Medellin that we cannot presuppose faith in members of the Church. Baptism is no guarantee that people have come to encounter Christ and adhere to him and the Church with their whole hearts. It does not guarantee deep communion with Christ.

The work at Medellin was landmark, and it came to be the turning point in our fuller understanding of catechesis. It summarized all the previous study weeks and led to the renewal that we now have in the Church.

Following Medellin, Pope Paul VI published the *General Catechetical Directory* (GCD) in 1971, which provided a framework on which a great deal of catechetical renewal was built. This directory reflected all the work done to that point at the various study weeks and at the Council. But the document contained a few lines in paragraph twenty which may have gone largely unnoticed by many. These lines, it turns out, helped set the stage for much that would follow:

> [Bishops] should remember that catechesis for adults, since it deals with persons who are capable of a fully responsible adherence, *must be considered the chief form of catechesis*. All other forms, which are indeed always necessary, are in some way oriented to it (emphasis mine).

Encounter with Jesus

A principal architect of this new approach with a focus on adults was Bishop Raymond Lucker. He was the main force behind it and the organizer of the effort to produce it. No bishop in the Church may have given as much careful thought to catechesis as Ray Lucker. Raised in both urban and rural settings in Minnesota, he was ordained in 1952 and assigned as an assistant director in the Archdiocese of St. Paul for the Confraternity of Christian Doctrine (CCD) office. He earned two doctorates, one in education at the University of Minnesota and one in theology in Rome. In his doctoral thesis for this latter degree (which was published as a book) Lucker gives a long, detailed history of catechesis, and he notes that after the reformation, catechesis became concerned with:

> ...knowledge of what we must believe in getting to heaven. And for the next four hundred years, one of the most important aims of religious education will be to equip the child to defend his faith against the attacks of the heretics [that is, the Protestants] and to answer their objections. (*The Aims of Religious Education, in the Early Church and in the American Catechetical Movement.* Rome, Italy: Catholic Book Publishing Co, 1966, p. 110)

The fundamental aims of teaching religion, however, he argued in this same doctoral thesis, must be:

> To develop a living, personal faith, to bring the students to complete conversion of life, to inspire commitment to Christ, and to help them enter into communion with God. The writer of this paper is in full accord with these aims (p. 222).

Ray Lucker later served as director of the Department of Education at the United States Catholic Conference, in Washington, DC. He was ordained an auxiliary bishop of the Archdiocese of St. Paul and Minneapolis in 1971 and later served for twenty-five years (to the day) as Bishop of the Diocese of New Ulm in Minnesota, where his own conversion to Christ played a central role in his extensive public teaching. He died of a melanoma on September 19, 2001.

Earlier in his life, Ray Lucker had fallen under the influence of Archbishop Edwin O'Hara who believed that the plan to have every child in a Catholic school did not serve the Church as well as some thought it would. Instead, O'Hara felt that "the greatest need in the Church was [for] an educated laity, people who were committed to their faith and were interested in handing it on to others" (Lucker in November 1994, in an address which was part of the St. Paul Seminary Centennial Lecture series. The paper he gave is archived at the University of St. Thomas. I take these notes from the paper written by William McDonough, which is cited in the acknowledgments.).

In 1964, Lucker co-wrote an essay with Theodore Stone in which they expressed strong belief in what was emerging as the new catechesis.

> [The historical development in catechesis] might give the impression that first comes instruction, then formation, and finally, the personal meeting between God and the student. The reverse, however, is more correct. Communion with God ordinarily does not take place at the end of the religion lesson, but rather whenever God approaches through sacred signs (biblical, liturgical, witness, or doctrinal signs)…to transform one's mentality. ("Formation and Training of Lay Catechists" in *Pastoral Catechetics.* New York: Herder and Herder, 1964, p 239)

Bishops from other nations such as England, Wales, and Canada also began laying the groundwork for an approach to catechesis that addressed more than children. Indeed, if we are to be successful with the children in the first place, we know that their parents must be involved in every level of faith formation! Without the parents, all our efforts amount to "seed falling on rocky ground." Faith will sprout because of our efforts, but the real harvest of faith can only be sustained within the home.

In 1974, an international synod of bishops dealt in great depth with the question of evangelization raised at Medellin, but they did not publish any outcomes. Instead, they encouraged Pope Paul VI to reflect on their findings, which he did, publishing an apostolic exhortation in 1975, *Evangelii Nuntiandi* or, in English, "On Evangelization in the Modern World." It was received with tremendous grace by the people of the Church. At the time, it was arguably the most important document issued in the Church since the close of Vatican II. It is concise (only five chapters long), vibrant, readable, and profound. In article four, the pope posed his leading question: "At this turning point of history, does the Church or does she not find herself better equipped to proclaim the Gospel and to put it into people's hearts with conviction, freedom of spirit, and effectiveness?"

Notice this question. It is a thoroughly modern concern, rooted in today's situation. It is challenging. It is Christ-centered and focused on the Gospel, the kerygma. And it is powerful: Do we have conviction? Is there freedom of spirit? And, mainly, are we *effective*?

And most importantly, this document marked a turning point for pastoral planners. Whereas in the past, the concern was for Catholics to be thoroughly familiar with the Church, its teachings, laws, liturgies, and traditions, now it seems the concern shifts to something more Christ-centered. *As a Catholic, do you know Christ? Have you experienced the life-changing power of an initial encounter with Christ?* In other words, have you been "converted?" Conversion to Christ of this sort, the *General Directory for Catechesis* would later argue, *precedes* catechesis (article 62).

This key turning point has led, of course, to decades of work on what we call "evangelization." For Catholics, this is a difficult term and yet another word with Greek origins. Catholics don't know much about conversion to Christ. It sounds vaguely "protestant" to us. And yet, if you examine the message of Pope John Paul II, the first pope in the Church after this document was promulgated, you'll find him to be profoundly Christ-centered. Everywhere he went in the world: at clergy gatherings, in meetings of men and women religious, in preparation for the Jubilee Year, at academic meetings, youth rallies, or masses for the throngs, his message was similar. "Come to Christ. Do not be afraid. Give your heart to Christ. Open wide the doors to Christ."

He saw Christ as the Lord of the universe and the center of all humankind. It was fundamental to him. It was an insight that he gained through the Spirit.

Pope Francis, of course, profoundly echoes all of this development. In the opening section of his first message to the world-wide Church, he said in #3:

> I invite all Christians, everywhere, at this very moment, to a renewed personal encounter with Jesus Christ, or at least an openness to letting him encounter them; I ask all of you to do this unfailingly each day. No one should think that this invitation is not meant for him or her, since "no one is excluded from the joy brought by the Lord." The Lord does not disappoint those who take this risk; whenever we take a step towards Jesus, we come to realize that he is already there, waiting for us with open arms.

In 1977, a second international synod of bishops met in Rome with catechesis as its focus, no doubt preparing to draw up that directory which had been called for in article forty-four of the document on bishops at the Council. Bishop Raymond Lucker attended this synod as one of four official delegates from the U.S. Conference of Bishops. While at the synod, Lucker gave a speech to the assembled bishops in which he said:

> [T]he most pressing need in the church is the evangelization and catechesis of adults [as] the *General Catechetical Directory* so forcibly reminded us....We have neglected the central goal of catechesis, which is to strengthen faith. And we have almost totally ignored the evangelization of the Catholic people....I say that the key to the catechesis of children and youth is the catechesis of adults. ("Needed: Adult Catechesis." *Origins* 7/18. Oct 20, 1977, 276-277)

But Lucker also made a key point which we now embrace as a vital step in successful catechesis for the whole community. In this same speech at the synod, he said:

> First...people come to an initial faith. They accept Jesus as Lord...and in a general way respond....We call this evangelization. Then comes catechesis, which presupposes this initial faith and is concerned with nurturing it, strengthening it, and making it mature.

Reflection
When you read Bishop Lucker's comments above, what strikes you most strongly about them? How do you connect them to the pastoral planning needs of your parish?

As the synod ended, the bishops issued a message to the people of God regarding their findings, and they also sent a set of resolutions to Pope Paul VI. Two years later, in 1979, Paul John Paul II issued the apostolic exhortation, *Catechesi Tradendae*, or in English, "On Catechesis in Our Time."

This exhortation laid the groundwork for a high-level renewal of catechesis in today's Church. It begins by reiterating what Paul VI had said earlier, catechesis is Christ-centered and it is rooted in tradition. Evangelization is the overarching activity, and catechesis is one dimension of that. The main sources, as directed by Vatican II's *Dogmatic Constitution on Divine Revelation*, are Scripture and tradition. It also treats various practical aspects of catechesis and concludes by saying, in essence, that catechesis isn't just for children; *it's for everyone.*

And of course, once again, this document proclaimed that the definitive aim of catechesis is "to put people not only in touch but in communion, in intimacy, with Jesus Christ," as Bishop Lucker had forcefully argued. Later in his own diocese, Bishop Lucker instructed his people in these words:

> Every parish…needs opportunities for adults to come together to pray, to witness to God's gifts in their lives, and to grow in the knowledge and love of Jesus. If this means that classroom instruction has to be suspended for a time while the teachers are being formed, so be it. Nothing can replace adult growth in faith (*Prairie Views: Twenty Five Years of Pastoral Letters*).

Then in 1997, with the approval of Pope John Paul II, the *General Directory for Catechesis* was published. Drawing on the wisdom and spirit of all the work mentioned above, and much that is not mentioned here for the sake of brevity, the GDC provides sound, workable principles on which we can base our current work in catechesis.

Whole community catechesis arises from the GDC. The name itself, "whole community" comes from article 254 where it says:

"The whole Christian community is the origin, locus, and goal of catechesis. Proclamation of the Gospel always begins with the Christian community and invites [people] to conversion and the following of Christ."

Chapter 4:
What Is Conversion?

We are not converted only once in our lives
but many times,
and this endless series
of conversions and inner revolutions
leads to our transformation.
Thomas Merton

Illustration: John and Mary Ellen
Note: This story is taken from **Promise and Hope: Pastoral Theology in the Age of Mercy** by Bill Huebsch, available from Twenty-Third Publications or Amazon.com.

When John called Mary Ellen, the pastoral associate in his parish, to set an appointment for pastoral counseling, she knew something had changed for John. His voice sounded upbeat, and their conversation was full of laughter and hope. She'd been accompanying John periodically since the death of his wife a year earlier. John and Dorothy had been married for thirty-eight years, and her death came after a long struggle with cancer. She was the love of his life, and this loss was devastating for him. Mary Ellen remembered him telling her once that losing Dorothy was like losing an arm in an accident. "'I've healed,'" he told her. "'I'm not bleeding anymore. But I know I'll never get my arm back.'"

John was a regular around the parish, often at daily Mass, and willing to help whenever called. But since Dorothy's death, everyone noticed that there were an abiding sadness and sense of loss. He was working through this in a regular series of chats with Mary Ellen.

Several months after the funeral, one of John's friends convinced him to participate in a weekend retreat. It was a three-day retreat held at a center where participants lodged together for the whole three days. He had never participated in this sort of thing, and John was reluctant about it, but his friend convinced him to do it, so off he went. The weekend consisted of talks, small group discussions, prayer, liturgy, and meals. To John's way of thinking, they didn't get enough sleep, but when he returned home on Sunday afternoon, it was clear to his children and others near him that something very important had changed.

What had changed? Well, to begin with, as when he saw his children after the retreat, he wanted to hug them! John hadn't exactly been the hugging type. He had been a dairy farmer most of his life, and he actually got closer to his cows every day than he did to his own children. But he'd been hugging people all weekend long at the retreat, so hugs it would be, all around, for everyone, even for his sons.

He brought home a Bible, in which he had been underlining phrases and marking them with a yellow highlighter. He had the Bible stuffed full of prayer cards and notes. And he was reading it every day! One of his sons actually asked him one day if he had maybe become Lutheran! To his son, reading the Bible was what Lutherans did. Catholics, he thought, owned Bibles but they never actually read them.

He came home with a deeper love for the Eucharist than he'd ever had in his life. On the retreat, the Eucharist was celebrated in a small small-group setting where they were standing near the altar, taking part in ways John had never done before.

But the big change was that he came home happy. Now, mind you, John was never actually unhappy. He was a friendly, well-met fellow, and people would have said he was always happy. But he'd also been dragged by Dorothy's illness through a terrible episode of loss. He was weary of carrying the sadness he felt at losing his partner. He wasn't chronically unhappy, but he had been severely tested.

So now in Mary Ellen's office, John began to tell her about the weekend. Among other things, he mentioned that he was continuing to connect with people from the retreat at local gatherings; he was continuing to read and study. She was surprised by this; John had been timid about such connections. Mary Ellen was curious about what brought about this transformation in John. Like everyone else, she could clearly see the new lightness of being and a strong sense of hope in him. So, she invited John to tell the story about how this all happened.

"Well, on the weekend," he began, "someone gave a talk on…" And then he used two words which that Mary Ellen had never heard coming from this fellow's mouth before—"…on the Paschal Mystery," he said. She was quite surprised to hear him use that term. Here was "plain old John" discussing the Paschal Mystery with her like it was a slice of daily bread. John saw her response but went on. "So, this speaker told us about how Christ lived and died with self-giving love, but how, really, there is a call embedded in everyday life for each one of us to do that. The speaker told us we would all be called in some way in our daily lives—maybe quite often—and invited to give of ourselves and empty ourselves for the sake of someone else. He said it would be a mystery which that we might not understand completely at the time, but that if we do enter into it and practice self-giving love, lo and behold, we will find there is a new life to live afterward. We will discover," he said, "that Jesus is walking with us in friendship, that we can turn our hearts to him, and that his grace would comfort and console us." John told her all this in one long, excited sentence. He was like someone who had just found something new and was so thrilled to have found it that he just couldn't stop talking about it and showing it to people.

Mary Ellen told me later that she was speechless in the face of all this. John continued. "So, after this talk, we were in our small group; the leader passed a crucifix around the circle and told us he'd like each of us to tell about a time when we experienced this chance to really die to ourselves. But he said that, if we wanted, we could just hold the cross and not talk, but just think quietly to ourselves. I guess he didn't want to pressure us to talk. Well, I made up my mind then and there that when it came around to me, I'd just do that. I'd just hold it and be quiet. But then people started sharing, and one said this, and another said that, and when it did finally come around to me, I just held that crucifix and looked at Jesus, and then I don't know what got into me, but I just started talking. I told them about Dorothy and all that happened with her, and all the sadness and all of it, and I suddenly realized, that was my call. I didn't see it at the time, but within her illness was embedded a summons for me: the chance to really love her. I knew right then that there that I'd have a new life after this. I just knew it."

"And then—this is the most remarkable part of it all— when we were at Mass that evening sitting quietly after Communion, I felt his presence, Jesus' presence, with me. I heard him tell me that he knew how much I suffered, that he understood about the loneliness of losing Dorothy, and that he was with me in this through these people, through my family, my parish…" and then he eyed looked at Mary Ellen and said, "and even through you, Mary Ellen. Right then and there I realized something so powerful that it brought tears to my eyes," John continued. "I realized that Dorothy may have died, but before she did, she saved me. She saved me."

A long silence hung in the room. Mary Ellen allowed it to simply be.

"See?" John explained to her finally, "This is the Paschal Mystery. It's not only about Jesus' death; it's about how we have to die. It's not only about him rising. It's about how we rise again from the ashes of our lives. And the thing is," he finished, "the patterns of dying and rising that I establish now in my life are going to be the patterns I take with me when I die. The love in our hearts is all that we take with us into the next life. That's what they told us."

Reflection

Do you know someone (maybe yourself) who has experienced this initial encounter with Christ, leading to deeper communion with God? Spend some time in the next month or so listening to the stories from such folks. Let it sink into your own consciousness how vitally important it is for people to begin their journey of faith with such a moment, as St. Paul also did on the road to Damascus.

On this retreat, John had what we call an "initial encounter with Christ." Even though he'd been baptized many years before and had been a church-going Catholic his entire life, this initial encounter now reshaped everything for him. And the initial encounter was sustained by the follow-up gatherings of others who'd also had that same experience. John had turned his heart to Christ, had turned toward the face of God, and had experienced true conversion.

This is the conversion about which Bishop Lucker was so personally convinced. Those who knew him were aware that he, too, had passed through such an initial conversion. It shaped everything he did in his ministry.

So what is this? What happens when someone experiences this initial turning of the heart to Christ?

We can't see it happen
We can't really see conversion happen, not in the same way that we watch a movie unfold, for example, or watch a ball game progress. Conversion is the work of the Spirit within us. We place ourselves in a position where an opportunity for conversion is possible, and the Spirit does the work.

Normally, the moment of conversion is linked to faith sharing. Somehow in talking about our faith with others, the Spirit touches our own hearts. It is personal, meaning that each of us experiences this at our own time and in our own way. But it is not private. Faith is shared, not hoarded. It is abundant, not scarce. And yet, we cannot really see it until we look back at those moments.

In the catechumenate, there is an ancient practice in the Church known as mystagogy. Here we have yet another word with its origins in Greek. It's worth understanding what this word means because it's the avenue to being able to recognize our own conversion. The word itself means something like, "reflecting on mysteries." The practice of mystagogy is to pause after an experience (of any kind; it needn't be overtly religious) recall the experience, and reflect on what touched your heart, what remains in your memory about this experience. Another way into mystagogy is to ask what struck me in this, what did I see or hear—or smell or touch? Mystagogy leads us to be able to see the signs of God's presence, even while we cannot see God.

Signs of conversion
So we look in our lives and the lives of those around us for *signs of conversion.* If we can see signs that the Spirit is moving and shaping us, then conversion is going on.

For example, conversion leads us to a supple sense of self, and we find we can adapt to the ebb and flow of life more easily. We come to understand that we need not cling too rigidly to the dock, but we can swim out into daily life with confidence and without fear. This is a sign that conversion is happening within us.

Another sign of conversion is growing flexibility with others. Just as we can sense ourselves bending with the Spirit, being more supple, so we allow others to have their own experiences too. We are less judgmental and more accepting. We find that those teachings of Jesus on the Mount are taking hold. Now they are more than mere words of Scripture, but an actual way of life for us: "Do not judge, so that you may not be judged" (Mt 7:1).

The third sign of conversion in our lives is a growing sense of generosity, with money, time, material things, and even with our own inner lives. Many times we begin to operate in life as though everything is scarce, and we must gather and hoard to have enough. But when we are in Christ, a trust overtakes us that changes that. Again, the teachings of Jesus take on a whole new and real meaning, "Give to everyone who begs from you, and do not refuse anyone who wants to borrow from you" (Mt 5:42).

A fourth sign might be that we grow in patience with others as they sort out their lives. We find ourselves forgiving freely when someone wrongs us. Forgiveness like this frees us more than the other. It allows us to let go and hold no grudge. These others who hurt or disappoint us can often become our "enemies." We hold them at arm's length, keep them at a distance. But when we experience conversion, we find that we are just less focused on all that. A certain grace of forgiveness sweeps in. This is a "given-ness" before the hurt. It's an *unconditional* attitude on our part that in Christ, the positive energy of love trumps the negative energy of dislike, indifference, or hate. We learn to forgive "seventy times seven times."

Another sign of conversion in our lives is that we find we have a stronger sense of hospitality toward others, strangers as well as friends. We find ourselves living with real day-to-day love for others, affirming them, loving them, and caring for them. This is genuine, not forced. It's a spontaneous expression of love, prompted by the Spirit within.

We also develop a heart for the materially poor. This is no small thing in the Gospels, which are packed with warnings about the dangers of wealth. "Do not store up for yourselves treasures on earth, where moth and rust consume and where thieves break in and steal," we are warned in Matthew 6:19-21. "But store up for yourselves treasures in heaven…for where your treasure is, there your heart will also be."

We become aware of our own failure and sin, and freely realize that we are, indeed, only earthen vessels. We grow into prayerful people. We see the events of daily life through the lens of the Gospel. We have a strong sense of the presence of God. We find deep, abiding joy. We see ourselves as part of the community of God. We celebrate the sacraments with new energy and life. We sing with a full voice. We see in others the very Christ in whom we believe. We get a sense of our own vocation to care for others and lead them to Christ. The list of signs goes on.

A key sign of conversion is a deep love for the Eucharist, not as a private devotion, but as that big, messy shared event we celebrate on Sunday mornings together. Parishes find that as members have this initial experience of conversion, their liturgies begin to soar! People sing with full hearts, and there is a strong sense of prayerfulness. The community feels united and purposeful. In short, the full, active participation called for at Vatican II comes into reality—as a result of being in a converted parish community.

Likewise, people who are in Christ are indeed just generous with both their money and their talents. People step forward because the Spirit living within them urges them to. They take more risks, are willing to give their time, and they do so with excitement rather than reluctance.

And finally, a sure sign of conversion is a *desire* for more faith formation. Once such an initial encounter is experienced, people want more. They now want to grow in their faith. The doldrums of parish life where no one seems interested are replaced with the high winds of keen interest in lifelong faith formation.

The challenge for the parish

Now to our point here regarding pastoral planning. The wonderful initial encounter with Christ, the experience of true conversion, sustained in the community, the kind John experienced—*that's what we want for every adult in the Church.* When that happens, the rest of the pastoral plan falls into place because the signs of that conversion lead to it. The poor are fed. The lonely are visited. The newcomer is welcomed to the faith. The rejected are loved. The widow, the orphan, and the stranger are taken in. The table is set for all. Everyone has the good news preached to them.

But, as I said above, we cannot assume that everyone in the parish has had this initial encounter with Christ. We cannot assume that conversion is going on around us. We cannot assume that merely because they are baptized, the members of the parish are "in Christ" in this way.

And yet, *we do assume this.* Most parishes have no pastoral plan that addresses conversion. And even fewer have a pastoral plan that addresses how to sustain that conversion throughout one's entire lifetime. Without a vision and plan, this key dimension of parish life often gets ignored. But ignoring it is precisely what Bishop Lucker knew would create a lackluster parish. Without a community of people who have met Christ, given their hearts to him, experienced this conversion, and see the signs of it in their lives, how can we expect them to be financially generous, prayerful, motivated to learn, or willing to volunteer?

Two big ideas

There are two parish activities that we know work to (1) help people grow closer to Christ (2) to help them sustain the fire of faith in their hearts over the long term. These are

- **Parish-based retreats** such as the Living Christ Retreat, the Christ Have Mercy Retreat, or others that are easy to implement, affordable to sponsor, and enjoyable for participants.
- For more information on a wonderful parish-based retreat called *Sanctus,* go to ThePastoralCenter.com and search for *Sanctus*.

- **Faith gatherings for adults** in the parish. These can be highly social times with a brief period of faith sharing added. They need not be difficult to organize. They could be held in the parish club or even in a local pub. It often helps to have a brief talk by an inspiring speaker. The keyword here in *brief.* Anything too long will kill this. The point of the gathering is to allow adults to have social time with faith sharing included.

A note about faith sharing: This isn't the same as "discussing theology." Faith sharing involves looking into one's heart to find how God may be speaking to us in the words of Scripture, in nature, in the love of our families, in the liturgy, or in other ways. The *sharing* part is vital. When we share faith, it becomes more real. It allows us to hear and see God more clearly as he stands beside us every day, as he walks with us in our lives, and as he calls us to be his loving, caring people. Whatever form these faith gatherings take, the sharing is essential.

Chapter 5
Writing the Plan

"Our goals can only be reached
through a vehicle of a plan,
in which we must fervently believe,
and upon which we must vigorously act.
There is no other route to success."
Pablo Picasso

OK, so we know we must build conversion of the heart into parish life for people to have the fire of faith which creates parishes that are active and attractive. But how do we plan? The steps are less complex than one might think.

Step 1. Decide to do this, commit yourself to the vision and process. Then get the right people to help.

The commitments of the parish priest and paid or volunteer pastoral workers are essential. Without that, you cannot proceed. Once you as a staff have reviewed the work of the past fifty years in the church, considered the current needs in your parish, and come to believe in the core work of helping people deepen their communion with Christ, then you must make your first decision.

As parish leaders, your own humility and modesty in sharing this decision with others in the parish will be powerful. By being "the deciders," you do not become the "dominators." You must be firm in your resolve and commitment, however. You must passionately desire the outcomes which the planning for this core work will produce. You must be ready to work tirelessly behind the scenes, attributing success to your leaders, but accepting failure as your own responsibility. You must also be ready to travel beyond what you know to be the comfortable and familiar territory of being a "good" parish.

A key meeting. When you're ready to do so, hold a key meeting with your top leaders—whether paid or volunteer—or both. In this meeting, make the formal decision to go forward. Mark this as your beginning point and anniversary. Later, when we evaluate and measure outcomes, this will be a key date in your planning process.

The key people. This may not be easy or even possible for you to do alone, which is why having the right team is so essential. So, the second step, after your own firm commitment to this is made, is to make sure you've got the right people traveling with you. Therefore, before you even begin the planning process, evaluate your "planning team." Parish teams tend to form accidentally. Some members of the team have been there since "three parish priests ago." Others have only just arrived. How long they've served matters less than whether they share in the dreams and visions of being a great parish.

Human resources in the church can be a real minefield. Hiring people and laying people off is not easy work. But it is important for you to fix firmly in your own mind the importance of having the right people in the right places on the staff. This will make the difference between remaining simply a good parish and becoming truly great! Even before the planning begins, who you have working and planning with you is far more important than what they are doing. This is especially true in parishes where no one has ever been paid except the parish priest—and this is more common than one thinks!

You can have the best plan and strategy in the world for your parish, but if you do not have the right people on the bus, as Jim Collins puts it, you'll never get where you're going. We sometimes think we're doing a favor for those "wrong" people who are already active in the parish. We think the charitable thing to do is to give them one more chance, or worse, find ways to have someone else do the tasks they aren't capable of doing. But in fact, the charitable thing, and the right thing for the parish is to help them find the true vocation where they can excel, even if it is outside parish ministry.

Discernment about the role and vocation to which we are called in the church must include all the things we are discussing here. We may be placing obstacles in front of the Spirit by failing to choose and form the right group of leaders.

Step 2. Identify and name someone to act as your coordinator.

It is now time to name the leader who will be responsible for implementing this plan. Note that in some parishes, this same person may also have responsibility for the children's religious education program. But in most cases, this will have to be a separate role simply because the workload would be too much if they were combined.

This coordinator may need to receive at least some compensation for his or her work. Working with the team, the coordinator operates as a sort of entrepreneur in the parish, helping to lead and invent the new horizons toward which the pastoral plan will stretch. Other characteristics to look for in this person might include:

- Understands well the task of helping people deepen their communion with Christ.
- Has the ability to share about his or her deep communion with Christ.
- Can be inventive, without running off alone in his or her own direction.
- Works well with others; is modest and humble, yet driven
- Is selfless and generous with time and can attend meetings and other gatherings, but at the same time can live a healthy, balanced life
- Is a very gifted teacher and a good communicator
- Has a sense of humor, including about him or herself
- Is deeply rooted in what is authentically Catholic
- Can plan with an eye to ecumenical relations

Part of the job description of this coordinator will be:

- To carry the plans designs of the team forward and help integrate those designs into parish life
- To make sure funding is there in the parish budget
- To balance new initiatives with other aspects of parish life

His or her job description might also include:

- Convene and coordinate the team

- Stay in constant close communication with the parish priest and the rest of the pastoral staff. There should be no surprises for the pastor and senior staff.
- Coordinate efforts among the various ministries of the parish, including very practical matters such as schedules and limited resources or the use of building space. This person would do the problem-solving needed from time to time, to keep the plan moving forward. He or she would watch for opportunities in the liturgical calendar, the culture, the neighborhood, and the town, and ask the question, "How can we take advantage of this opportunity?"
- He or she would also ask the question, "Who isn't being served?"
- This person would also assist in creating the annual calendar and making sure there are space and equipment where needed.

This coordinator is also the person who can help keep the parish from being too timid. Starting too slowly is like not starting at all. There may be a time when as a parish, you simply decide that this is the direction and now is the time—so let's get started! Having a great coordinator in place makes that possible.

Step 3. Identify and gather a team to shape and design opportunities for conversion in the parish.

This is the group who will both plan and implement the vision for lifelong faith formation. Who should be on this team?
- The parish priest and possibly other priests on the staff
- Persons who will be responsible for carrying out the plan
- Key volunteers, retired members of the staff who still live in the parish, ministry leaders, and others.

You're looking for people who are deeply committed to the dreams and visions of the parish, but without their own agenda. Like the other leaders described here, they should be modest, yet driven.

The task of the team is to implement the steps that follow.

Step 4. Identify and talk with the specific groups you hope to reach within the parish

The planning team has two major roles. The first major role (we'll discuss the second role a bit later) is to identify and talk with all the various constituencies within the parish, and have in mind all the various needs and wants of these groups. Much of the team's work is to address those needs. Here is a list of such groups in any given parish. Your specific parish may have more or less.

- Parents or guardians who have children in religious ed or the school
- Adults who do not have children in catechesis
- Catechumens and candidates for full communion
- Those returning to the church after being away a while
- Those who remain distant from the parish
- Parish council members and members of various parish committees
- Catechists, school teachers, and their aides
- Lectors and liturgical musicians, the choir
- Those with special needs and disabilities
- Confirmation students
- Students on campuses within the parish
- Young adults—out of secondary school but not in the military or higher education
- Small Christian communities
- Selected households in the parish

- Maturing adults living in assisted care facilities in the parish

The listening process
It's important for the members of the planning team to actually meet the members of the parish in person. Knowing about people is very different from being personally familiar with them. This process of meeting parishioners must occur throughout the years ahead. It's not something that can be initiated and completed in a month or two. Members of the team make it a point to seek out and talk with the members of the parish as often as possible.

Step 5. Hold a series of meetings as a team over about six months.

The second major role of the team is the actual planning work itself. The typical planning process used in parishes calls for a series of meetings over the course of about six months. There is no better or worse time of year to begin this process. It's simply best to begin when you are ready. Each meeting will follow a similar format, but with an ever-developing and expanding agenda. The actual meeting agendas are outlined just below, but the general format includes:
- Gathering with hospitality
- Spending about twenty minutes (depending on the size of your team) in faith formation for yourselves. Proclaim a small part of the Gospel reading from the upcoming Sunday liturgy. Go around the circle and share how this story or incident in Jesus' life touches you. What does it say to your parish at this time?
- After the sharing, invite brief spontaneous prayer from the members. End the opening prayer with the Hail Mary and begin your work.

- Close with more hospitality. (You can never get too much!)
- In each meeting during this month's, the team deals with the following points:

Meeting One: "What are we doing now?"

1) Working through the list of groups above, ask yourselves this question: What is the state of each group relative to our core work? In other words, how does the parish help the members of each of these groups come to a closer friendship with Jesus?

- What do we offer them now?
- How is what we offer received by members of each group?

As you discuss these questions group by group, remember to keep refining your list. For example, as you work with the group "parents or guardians who have children in religious ed or the school," you may find that you want to be more specific for your purposes. You might consider subgroups such as:

- School parents
- Religious ed parents
- Single parents
- And so forth

2) The second issue for planning at this meeting is related to this. What have we tried that has succeeded and what have we tried that has failed within each group? What have we done in the past to include each of these groups in the heart of the parish? What have we done or failed to do in terms of helping people deepen their communion with Christ and to sustain that in the church?

The results of this first meeting are usually very affirming and positive for the parish. Most parishes have many excellent initiatives underway already on which to build toward greatness!

Before you adjourn to refreshments and social time, be sure to consolidate your discussions into a single, brief report. This report and summary should be shared widely in the parish as soon as possible after the meeting.

Meeting Two: "What outcomes do we want to see in the future?"

1) Having read the material in *Setting the Church on Fire*, and knowing what the popes and bishops have been calling us to over the past fifty years, not to mention the insights of your own neighbors and parishioners, identify clearly together *what you want to occur in your parish*. The question on your agenda should read: What outcome do you want to see for each of the affected groups in this parish? What do you want to occur in the lives of these folks as a result of parish ministry? What do you want people to get from all our efforts as a parish?

Your temptation is to be too general here. But make the list of outcomes for each group quite specific. For example, with "parents who have children in religious ed or the school," you might be tempted to say that you want them to love Christ and be active in the church. Well, okay. Of course, you want that. But more specifically, there are other things you want for this group:

- To be able to speak articulately about their faith at home
- To know how to pray as a household
- To be able to understand and pass on the social teachings of the church
- And so forth

As you do this work over the coming weeks and months, plan to continually revisit your desired outcomes to shift them and tweak them until they are downright realistic.

Before you adjourn to refreshments and social time, be sure to consolidate your discussions into a single, brief report. This report and summary should be shared widely in the parish as soon as possible after the meeting.

Meeting Three: "What specific steps should we take to reach our desired outcomes?"

This is a key meeting. In the past two meetings, we have discussed 1) how we've done in the past and 2) what we hope the outcomes to be in the future for each of the groups within the parish. Now it's time to ask this question: What's next? What do we dream for our parish? Given our parish facilities, our history, the culture of our parish community, and so forth, what specific new programs do we want to offer? How will parish-based retreats and adult faith gatherings become part of parish life?

One way to surface these ideas is to simply and quickly list them on a black or whiteboard in your meeting room. Allow everyone's idea to be added to the list. As you make this first list, there are no "bad" or "good" ideas.

Once you have this list compiled, go back through it together as a group and start grouping various similar items together. Give each group a name. You might end up with five or six major groups or areas of planning.

Then begin sketching what the details of each group might look like and what next steps might be needed. At this point, you have not adopted anything as your plan, but you're only working with potential ideas. Some of the specific concrete steps needed to move each group forward might include

- Who will do this?
- Where will this happen?
- How much will this cost?
- Who will this serve in the parish?
- When could something like this begin?
- And so forth

Before you adjourn to refreshments and social time, be sure to consolidate your discussions into a single, brief report. This report and summary should be shared widely in the parish as soon as possible after the meeting. Be careful when speaking of these specific ideas in the parish that you make sure everyone understands that they're still only proposals at this point—not decisions!

Meeting Four: "Evaluate what we've done so far and define the solid ideas that emerged."
The purpose of this meeting is twofold. 1) The first is to pause in the planning process and review what you've done so far. Revisit it all step by step. And in this particular meeting, this is the question for your agenda: How has what we've done so far helped to advance the core work of the parish? Have we been too timid, or too ambitious?

2) The second part of the agenda for this meeting is to talk through those specific programs outlined in the last meeting, revisiting them with an eye to being realistic, yet challenging for the parish. How would the new plan for this parish look, drawn and detailed? The parish priest and the coordinator assist this part of the agenda by doing some preliminary work before the meeting. They should take the set of ideas generated at the last meeting and consider them with an eye to their reasonableness, realism, and potential to help the parish do its core work.

The work of the group in this meeting is to define a set of "proposed goals" along with the actions needed to implement them in the parish.

Implementing this plan begins immediately, or has most likely already begun. A plan based on dreams and visions in a parish really doesn't have a final form. The planning really doesn't end, and implementing certain parts of the plan can start as soon as they are seen as valuable. In fact, implementing various dimensions of the plan affects future outcomes. As more and more people are in ever deeper communion with Christ and on fire in their hearts, the plan itself changes and shifts. This is driven not by a fixed way of doing things, but by the Spirit, which "blows where it wills."

Therefore, the question on this meeting's agenda might be something like this: For the moment, as a team, what do we recommend for the parish? What first steps should we take, or have we already taken?

Once a basic first version of the pastoral plan is written and the calendar is complete, the team turns its attention to budgets, implementation, monitoring progress, brainstorming to solve problems, and support for the staff and parish priest. Continue to meet monthly or bimonthly, and continue to keep the process rolling forward.

Step 6. Prepare a short, written pastoral plan document.

Because they must unfold in real-time to be effective, the format for a written pastoral plan is based on the calendar. No pastoral plan will work that is not calendar-friendly! So as you choose each element to add to the plan, see how it might fit into the parish or school calendar. In the end, the plan document you write will be an actual calendar, fleshed out with various offerings. Don't forget this key principle: sometimes, when you add new dimensions to your pastoral plan, old ones must be removed. I know this can be painful for some folks, but we are in the process of shifting gears as a parish to add those two new elements: opportunities for conversion and adult faith formation to sustain that conversion.

The actual writing of the plan for the parish should be done by individuals, not by a team. In preparing the written report of the plan, be sure to keep it brief but complete. You might break down the various ideas into the following categories to help readers get perspective:

* Major initiatives
* Minor initiatives
* Things to stop doing
* Ideas tabled for now

Under each initiative, it helps readers to know a bit of detail, but use bullets and short descriptions rather than giving every detail. It might be wise to post a complete, detailed report on your parish web site for those who want to read it, while creating a much shorter version for use in the next step.

Step 7. Launch.
How you launch a pastoral plan such as this one is important. Start slowly. If you try to launch it all at once, it might be hard to manage. But if you go too slowly, no one will notice. The critical mass of a pastoral plan is the powerful new spirit it instills in the life of the parish. Once that spirit gets flowing, the process of starting up new initiatives is much easier!

We want to build a solid foundation here for the future of the parish, but there will not come a point where you can say to yourself, "Well, good, the planning is done so let's inaugurate the plan." In fact, the planning process is never complete. In fact, you may do more harm than good by setting a starting date and holding a kick-off celebration. That might work for a building-fund drive, but not for lifelong formation.

As I just suggested, there are two possible ways to sabotage the implementation of the plan. The first is by starting too fast, throwing out old programs and replacing them with new ideas that few people understand. People resent losing programs with which they are comfortable and familiar. Wouldn't you? So a gradual start is best, under the guidance of the parish priest and coordinator. Simply launch the first initiative by scheduling the first parish-based retreat, for example, without a lot of fanfare. It only takes a small crew and three rooms. Invite people to it. There's no need to advertise it as a "major new initiative" in the parish. As the first retreat is being planned, launch another initiative and plan for the first faith gathering, to give those forty new retreatants (and many others) a place to gather to sustain their faith. So begin gradually and without too much fanfare. Simply start launching your initiatives one at a time.

The second way to sabotage this plan is to move too slowly and timidly. If you say to yourself, "Well, okay, yes, this is our core work, but we'll only schedule one retreat for this year. And we'll put off the faith gatherings until next year." You really aren't launching enough balloons to be noticed under a plan with this kind of rollout schedule. That might be too slow a start. You really aren't implementing the plan unless you include all the elements that hold it together. Picking and choosing this or that element looks disorganized and it will be hard for you or anyone in your parish to see any difference from the current situation.

This process goes on forever. We keep finding new and better ways to help people grow in friendship with Jesus and in following his teachings. Success is in the striving, not the arriving.

What a fantastic period of history this is for the Catholic Church! After nearly seventeen centuries, the popes and bishops, working under the inspiration of the Holy Spirit, have restored the liturgy and the catechumenate to full use in the church.

Building on that, and having listened closely to God's people, those same leaders have now set the stage for us to re-invigorate the Church by creating opportunities for the same Holy Spirit to touch hearts and lives and deepen communion with God, in the context of parish life through parish-based retreats and other encounters. And we are now planning to do that! How wonderful for the Church! We are planning to help folks deepen their friendship and communion with Christ.

At the same time, we're planning to provide our people with a simple way to sustain that conversion, through faith gatherings for people of all ages and all stages of life! We have the know-how, the people, the will, and the resources to do this with tremendous success.

Bonus Material:
Parish Examination of Consciousness

Becoming aware of your particular parish culture

Parishes vary widely in terms of how conscious they are of the culture which drives parish life. To get an idea what the culture of your parish is like, you might start asking people this question: How do we do things around here? How you do things reflects your parish culture. It's often hard to put your finger on just what style of parish you may be, but looking back over your shoulder at how the parish responds to people, events, and new ideas really reveals a great deal.

For example, (1) what does the parish emphasize? Does it focus on welcoming people? On running efficiently? On meeting people's needs? On being innovative and new? Are members of the parish sharing faith often? Are they experiencing the happiness of knowing Christ personally? Are they bringing their daily lives to the table? Or is everything much more private than that?

(2) What does the parish expect of its people? Does it call people to strong, informed participation? Does it ask people for a lot—or just a little? Does the parish priest provide most of the ministry, or does the staff call the average people into ministry? When called, do people respond?

(3) What is the sense of possibility in the parish? Is yours a parish where people tend to say, "We tried that, and it didn't work"? Or is there a sense of optimism and hope that "If we build it, they will come"?

(4) What perceptions do people have of the parish, not only the perceptions which members have but also your neighbors in the community where you're located, including non-Catholic churches? Do people think of you as closed and taking care of your own? Or do they perceive you as reaching out to the world around you? Are you progressive? Traditional? Middle of the road? Are you perceived to be energetic as a parish, or lackluster?

(5) Do you allow your leaders to challenge you in their homilies, teaching, and administrative work? Or do you prefer as a parish to maintain the attitudes and practices as you always have?

An important exercise for the team.
One way to explore what your culture is like is to talk through the parish "examination of consciousness," which is below. It will help you see what you pay attention to and what you don't. Little by little, you'll start to note what constitutes your particular parish culture. I recommend that you draw together people who know the parish well and have lived in it a long time as well as folks who are new to the parish. Who should be invited? Certainly, the parish priest —you really can't proceed without him. Also invite core team members, volunteers, and other active members

of the parish. It may also benefit you to have one or two inactive members there, people who are just on the fringe of parish life. Their insights and wisdom may be very helpful to you. Likewise, be sure to include one or two young adults from the parish in this group. They will bring wisdom not only because of their status in the parish but also because youth ministry has always understood the journey to holiness so well.

Sit down together to share a brief evening prayer, a casual meal, and maybe a bottle of wine. After eating push back the dishes or move to a more comfortable space and "compare notes" as honestly as possible about your parish culture. You may use the questions in our "examination" but don't be limited by them.

The process of "comparing notes" has four steps in it, after the group has shared prayer and a meal. It helps to have someone designated as a facilitator for this. Many parishes invite an outside facilitator to assist them to allow the whole group of parish leaders to participate more fully in this process. There are several "styles of being parish" for you to consider. Many parishes find they have parts of them all; try very hard to identify which style you and the other parish leaders believe tends to be most prominent. After the process, you will be invited to share your dreams and visions about what you want the parish culture to evolve into. How exciting!

It would be most helpful if everyone present could read this entire booklet beforehand.

Parish Examination of Consciousness

Step one

Slowly read aloud the description for each of the seven styles. Rotate readers in your group for each style. Ask each participant to write down his or her first and immediate responses to each style in light of how accurately it describes your parish. The question is, "How much is this principle reflected in the culture of our parish at the present time?"

Participants should both rate it on a scale of one to five such as this one:

     1   2   3   4   5
----not at all-----somewhat-----very much in our culture----

As you go, ask each participant to make notes to explain how each decided on the rating. We want to tap into people's unfiltered views and observations of the parish.

Step two

When you have read them all go around the group inviting everyone to speak about their observations. Take each style in turn until you have talked about them all. This should be more of a conversation than a series of soliloquies.

- Of course, all comments should be given with charity, but that doesn't mean speakers can dodge the reality or "sugar coat" their comments. There are no right answers. This isn't a test. This is a way to compare notes on how people experience parish life.

- Have someone record all the scores for each possible style of parish culture. Take out the highest and lowest score for each and average the remainder.
- It helps to use a flip chart, smart screen, or shared note pad to write down the "big thoughts" people express as they explain their rating. As others add comments and agree, disagree, or expand on ideas, add that to the notes.

Step three

Take a brief refreshment break after everyone has spoken. Then return to the task. First, share the average scores. Then pull out of the comments the key ideas that describe your parish culture. One way to distill this information is to ask of the group:

- What struck you in what you heard here today?
- Which comments or ideas surprised you? Which did not?
- If you could summarize our parish culture in five to ten words, how would you describe it?

Step four

In closing, try to reach a consensus about what sort of parish culture people would like to see develop here? One way to do this is to ask questions like these:

- As you listened to all this, which styles of parish were most appealing to you?
- What would you like this parish to grow into?
- What factors unique to this parish prevent us from growing into a culture of holiness? How can we overcome these?
- Describe how you would like to see this parish in five years.

Seven Styles of Being Parish

Visionary? Are we a visionary parish? Are we seeking new ways to meet needs and pushing the envelope a little to do that? Is change common? Do people expect to hear about new initiatives often? Are we welcoming or addressing new groups with new needs? Who does not feel welcome at this time?

1   2   3   4   5
----not at all-----somewhat-----very much in our culture----

Comments and observations about the parish related to this style:

Administrative? Are we an administratively strong parish? Do we have well-oiled schedules, structures, and programs? Do we focus on meeting norms and standards for sacraments, membership, or preaching? Do we employ people to coach our leadership structure to make sure there are enough checks and balances in it, and that people understand group dynamics? Are we considered an efficient parish? Do we get all the work done on time?

1   2   3   4   5
----not at all-----somewhat-----very much in our culture----

Comments and observations about the parish related to this style:

Pastoral? Are we a pastorally-centered parish? Are fellowship and hospitality our main aims? Are we eager to welcome and make people a priority in parish life, meeting their needs by whatever structures work for them? Are we a parish that is known for our generosity and for meeting people's needs?

1   2   3   4   5
----not at all-----somewhat-----very much in our culture----

Comments and observations about the parish related to this style:

Ministry-centered? Are we a ministry centered parish? Do we encourage everyone to see him or herself as part of the common priesthood of the baptized and undertake ministry work? Do we prepare people for this ministry, in the parish, in the home, or in the society?

1   2   3   4   5
----not at all-----somewhat-----very much in our culture----

Comments and observations about the parish related to this style:

Holiness? Are we a conversion parish, one in which people share faith-based on encounters with Christ and each other? Do we give people chances for faith sharing and prayer, opening their hearts to the Spirit and then allowing the Spirit to grow in the often-surprising ways that the Spirit prompts? Do we help people hear the call to self-giving love, which is embedded in a hundred daily events of their lives?

           1   2   3   4   5
----not at all-----somewhat-----very much in our culture----

Comments and observations about the parish related to this style:

Neighborhood? Are we a well-connected neighbors-and-families parish? Do we have long-standing members who were part of the founding families and continue to lead and support the parish today?

           1   2   3   4   5
----not at all-----somewhat-----very much in our culture----

Comments and observations about the parish related to this style:

Made in the USA
Coppell, TX
31 October 2021